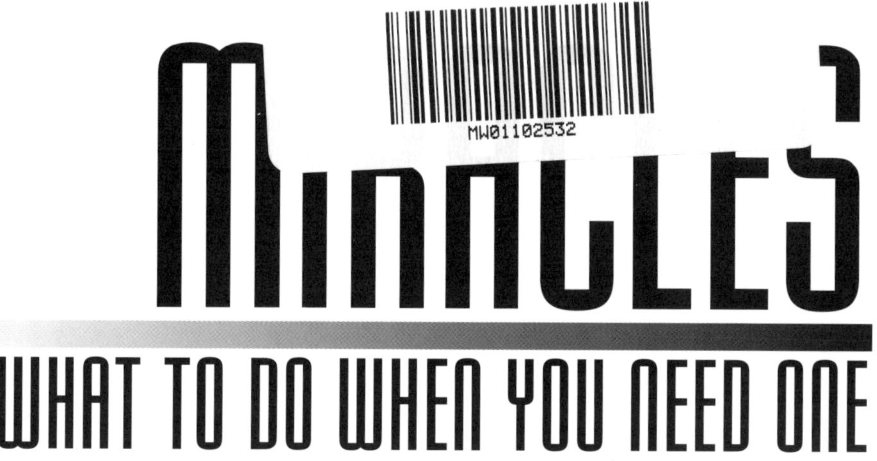

DR. DAVE MARTIN

Unless otherwise indicated, all Scripture quotations are taken from the New International Version.

Miracles
ISBN #0-9700987-3-1

Published by Favor International
P.O. Box 608150
Orlando, Florida 32860

FAVOR HONOR ROLL

Sade Abifarin
Funmi Adeleke
Adeyemi Adewole
Pastor Bayo & Olufunmilayo Adewole
Jessica Adriel
Ayoade Olusola Akere
Pastor Kore & Elizabeth Akindele
Olu Akinrinmade
Charisse Ala
Keith Alan St. Cyr.
Kari Alexander
Robert & Rosalie Allen
Rosemary Alvarez & Sons
Pastor Jay & Geri Amea
Jacqueline Anderson
Lamont & Leigh Anderson
Laide Animashaun
Tunde, Funmi, & Oyin Anjorn
David & Glory Arndt
Peggy Arnold
Bernard & Celeste Arrington
Denise Ashley
Adekunle & Olufunke Awojobi
Felicia Ayeni
Asonta Baker
N.L. Baker
Todd & Teri Bartel
Chris & Donna Bernard
Manny & Rogeitte Bernardino
Hope Bethune
Donald & Jessica Blankenship
Leo Bogee Jr.
Joan Bonvicini
Pastor Kendall & Starla Bridges
Larry & Barbara Broussard
Aaron & Rachel Broussard
Louise Brown
Normaline Bryan
John Budi
David & Sonja Burgess
T.R. & Jeanne Burke
Thomas & Gail Bush
Kevin & Alicia Cannady
James & Alverne Cannady
Kimeka Campbell
Tosin Ojo-Carons
Thomas & Ann Cartwright
Brenda Kay Carr
Jacqueline Casco
Adonye Chamberlain
Debra C. Chatman
Jim & Patty Childress
Benedicta Chidueme
Eartha Clarke
Gary & Kimberly Clayback
Bruce & Karen Clingan
Lisa Colello
Dwayne Conyers
Dr. Tim & Betty Cornett

Roberta Cortez
Derrick & Karen Countryman
Lucia Cox
Darlene Curry
Jessie, Peggy, & Marshall Craig
Ron & Carolyn David
Antonio Davila
Chad Davis
James & Shirley Davis
Pastor Mark & Hortensia Davis
Ronald & Barbara Deyka
John Dilemme
William & Cris Dorough
Ronald & Barbara Doyka
Remilekun Ayodeli-Duyle
Mayreen Easting
Angelee Ebbitt
Julian & Suze Edgar,
DJ & Cindy Edmonston
Donald & Renee Ellis
Bill & Barbara Etheridge
Aderomola Fabayo
Shawn & Doris Fogle
Patricia Formby
Arvis & Darlene Foshee
Paul Fournier
James Frankel
Gail Freeman
Pastor Henry W. Furr
Dennis & Ann Galbraith
Judith Galindo
Adedute A. Gbadehan
Harold & Ramona Gilbert
Landon & Carla Gilliland
Levon Goins
Dulce Gonzalez
Janie Gonzalez
Milagros Gonzalez
Shawn Gordon
Timothy & Linda Gorman
Nahshon & Rachel Graumann
John & Cassandra Grayson
David & Kathy Green
Joe & Angie Grosso
Danny & Sheryl Gurwell
Roger & Shanna Habich
J.L. Hagerman
Danny Hannes Sr.
Toni & Frederick Harbor
James Harris
Darlington & Colieen Hart
Robert & Ann Hartman
John & Nellie Harvey
Emil & Lisa Hawkins
John & Laura Hein
Andrew Hendriksen
Sheila Hentz
Ron & Cora Hernandez
Ronald & JoNell Henry
Tricia Henry

Jo Hewell
Peg Hill
Richard & Cathey Hill
Shal-Mar Hill
Richard & Susan Hinds
Brian & Judy Hood
James & Myrna Horne
Richard and Michelle Hornsby
Kevin & Amy Hunt
Clinton & Michelle Hunter
The Jones Family
Abimbola Idowu
Abiodun Johnson
Brett & Maria Johnson
Judy Johnson
Pastor Anthony Jones
Elsie Kaahaaina
Nani, Ui, the Kealoha Children &
Verlene Kaaiwela
Reginald & Brenda-Lee Kalahiki
Michael & Kimberly Kane
Pastor David & Deborah Katina
John & Ivy Kauth
Darci Kilbourn
Sandra Kinsey
George & Neoma Knox
James & Penny Kressman
Brain & Gretchen Kropp
Barbara Kuester
Pastor John & Betty Larsen
Kimberly Lascano
Samantha Leary
Keith Legg
Beverly Lee
Evelyn Leonard
Jane Lippy
Terry & Susan Locke
S. Michael & Nancy Lucius
Ralph & Nancy Ludlam
Vivian P.A. Mack
Jetina & Theresa Madison
Adesike Majolagbe
Carol Martin
Alex Ofosu-Mensah
Leila Merriweather
Bill & Nell Metcalf
Kalani & Jadeen Meyers
Moses McCutcheon Jr.
Shawn & Linda McNerney
Ronnie Mitchell
Theresa Morrison
Eric & Linda Mullins
Liza Munoz
Jeff Munson
Dr. Fred Musser
Dr. Simon & Mrs. Princess Ndekwe
Diane Ndjeunga
Gloria Negbenebor

FAVOR HONOR ROLL

William Douglas Norris
Ronald Nyamwaya
Atinuke Ogunsalu
Alfred & Bola Ojejinmi
Ijeoma Ojiaku
Abimbola Okubanjo
Linda Olale
Ayodeji Amos Olasupo
Patricia Heller-Olvera
Okey & Chidi Onyemelukwe
Aurea Ortiz
The Pagett Family
George Parker
Julia Parton
Robert & Margaret Perez
Gwendolyn Person
Hazeline Pilgrim
TAJ Poth
Beverley Powell
Pastor Tim & Kim Rankins
Kathy Rayburn
Rebecca Renfro
Jennifer Rice
Ken & Tammy Roberts
Mr. & Mrs. Dennis Robinson
Mike & Elaine Rogers
Fred & Vivian Ross
Diana Sanchez
Cecil Y Y Sarpong
Marquis & Mona Sartell
Ronald & Bonnie Setters
Deborah Shelton
Tommy & Kendal Shelton
Sandra Simpson
Amanda & Teresa Schreve
Carl Scott
Keith & Annette Screen
Elsie Simms
Debra Simon
Reginald Smith
Pastor Larry & Tamara Smoot
William E. Staubs
Cheryl Stevenson
Pastor Alvin Stewart ,Jr.
Candida Stewart
Kim Stingo
Laura Svetich
Tonya Sykes
J.R. & Sheila Talton
Tammy Thomas
Joesph & Ernestine Thompson
Jerry Tieman
John Tipton
Richard & Cynthia Tomsic
Gloria Tucker
Omotola Uwaifo
Nadine Valenzuela
Charles Vance
Joe & Billie Verdecchio
Carl & Sue Ann Warren
Carol Watler
Deji West
Jason Whitfield
Mark & Katie Williams
Ed, Darla & Whitney Williams
Charles & Lucretia Williams
Antjuan & Joan Wilson
Brad, Katy, & Riley Woods
Mercy Myles-Worgas
Deer Run & Co. LTD
Youth Challenge International
School of Ministry
Edward & Brenda Zimbardi

FAVOR
BLESSING
INCREASE

WHY I WROTE THIS BOOK

We all need miracles. I need miracles, you need miracles. There's something that every one of us is believing for God to do.

I'll never forget the day I heard Dr. Mike Murdock say, "You're never as far from a miracle as it first appears". What is a miracle? Miracles may mean one thing to one person and something totally different to someone else. The Webster dictionary says that a miracle is an event or an action that apparently contradicts known scientific laws. It's also defined as a remarkable thing. We serve a God of miracles. You are a miracle. The very fact that you're breathing right now is a miracle. The day you were born, a miracle happened. Your body is a miracle. The way it works is a miracle. Blood pumping through your veins, your heart beating, your lungs breathing, all that is a miracle. Miracles are happening all around you. When I think of a miracle I think of a supernatural intervention of God in the problems of your life.

In this book I want to help you reach and receive the miracle you're believing for. It may be a financial miracle, a miracle of healing, a family miracle, or a miracle in your marriage. I don't know what it is you're believing for, but I believe if you read this book and discover the principles and keys outlined in this book you will unlock the door to many miracles in your future.

I'm going to give you eight powerful keys to receiving your miracle. These are things that have worked for Christine and myself. They have been tried and tested and they work. Whatever the miracle is I know that these keys will help you unlock the door to your miracle. It doesn't matter if it is a financial miracle, a healing, or restoration in a relationship…all things are possible.

When I traveled with Pastor Benny Hinn I would see people that would drive hundreds of miles to a crusade to receive a miracle. The atmosphere of faith was strong and powerful. People were ready to receive; yet they would leave and lose the miracle that they got. I want to teach you not only how to receive a miracle but how to keep to the miracle that you've received; practical information that you can use today. Why would you wait another day for the answer for the miracle that you could receive today?

I heard Oral Roberts say one time, *"Miracles are coming toward you or going past you every day. All you have to do is take hold of yours."* I want to help you take hold of the miracle you're believing for. You'll read testimonies in this book of miracles that have happened in other people's lives. Remember, God is no respecter of persons; what he does for one person he can do for another. When you read those miracles, let it build up your faith to know if God can do it for them, God can do it for me. If God can get you out of debt, God can get me out of debt. If God can heal Mr. Johnson's cancer then God can Mrs. Smith's cancer. Whatever he does for one, he'll do for another. Get ready to receive. Put these principles to work in your life because I believe that your miracle is on its way.

Now I want you to focus your faith toward one thing. You may have several miracles that you need right now, but I want you to focus. What is on your mind the most? What do you go to bed praying for God to do? I want you to think about that one thing as you read the pages of this book and get ready for the manifestation.

FOCUS YOUR FAITH TOWARD ONE THING.

Think about that one thing as you read the pages of this book and get ready for the manifestation!

TABLE OF CONTENTS

CHAPTER

MIRACLES

NAME YOUR MIRACLE

CHAPTER ONE

Name Your Miracle

When you need a miracle from God, the first thing you've got to do is know what the miracle is you need. As you read this book, I want you to think of one miracle, the one thing that is on your mind more than anything else, the thing that you need God to do. There may be six or seven things that you're believing God to do, but I want you to focus your faith today toward one miracle. The first thing you've got to do is know what it is you want and be specific.

A ship never picks up its anchor until it has a destination.

A lady came up to me after service one night and wanted me to pray for her. She had her mortgage and a couple of other things that were due and she didn't have the money. She said, "I need more money." I said, "What do you need?" She said, "I need more money." I said, "How much more?" She said, "I need more, I've got these bills..." and I said, "Well how much are they altogether, how much do you need?" She didn't know the exact amount she needed. If she just needed more money then I could've given her a dollar and she would've had more money. Be specific. Know what it is you need from God.

Marilyn Hickey asked a friend of mine one time who was believing for a wife; she asked if he had ever made a list of all of the things he wanted in a woman? He said, "No, I've never made a list." She said, "Why don't you go back to your hotel room tonight and make a list of all of the things you want in a woman." He went back to his room that night and he got out his pen and paper and he began to sit down and write a list of all the things he was believing for, one after another. The next morning he arrived at the meeting and he and Marilyn were in the back talking. Marilyn asked him, "Did you make a list of all the things you want in a woman?" He said, "I did." Marilyn asked to see it and the man reached in his pocket and pulled out four pages of paper. She said, "My goodness, four pages of paper, that's a lot. Did you show it to God?" and he said, "I did". She said, "What did God say?" He replied, "God said if he could find a women like that, he'd probably get married himself!" We need to be specific, but we also need to be realistic. Marilyn said to him,

"Remember, God's just as concerned about her happiness as he is yours."

You can't leave where you are until you decide where you'd rather be.

The first thing you've got to do is know what the miracle is that you need. I can go to the Orlando airport and there's airplanes flying to different cities and locations all over the country but they don't sell me my ticket based on where I am. They sell me my ticket based on where I want to go. I can stand in the Orlando airport all day, watching planes fly all over the country, but until I decide where I want to go I'm going to stay at the airport in Orlando. I've got to choose a destination so I can leave the place where I am.

The first thing you've got to know is what it is you need from God. When I was trying to get out of debt, I could tell you to the exact penny what I needed to get out of debt. As I paid off bills, I kept up to the exact penny and could always tell you what I needed until the day I was debt free.

The first key to receiving your miracle is knowing what the miracle is that you need or you're believing for God to do.

MIRACLES

FIND SCRIPTURE

CHAPTER TWO

Find Scripture

The next thing I do when I need a miracle is I find in the Word of God where it says that I can have the miracle that I'm believing for. I find the scripture that promises me the answer.

"God is not a man, that He should lie."
— Numbers 23:19

My mom had a magnet on her refrigerator when I was growing up that said, 'God said it, I believe it and that settles it!' If you can find it in His Word, then you can believe it. If you believe it and stand on it, it can be done in your life. I don't pray, "Lord, if it be your will, heal my body." No, because I know His Word says, in 1 Peter 2:24, *"by His stripes you were healed".* I already know that it is His will. I don't have to pray, "Lord, if it be your will, bless me financially." No, I know His Word says in III John 2, *"I wish above all things that you would prosper and be in health as you soul prospers".* I know the Word of God. I know where it says if I'm believing for family members to get saved. Acts 16:31, *"believe for you and your whole household to be saved".*

I find in the Word of God where it says I can have the miracle because if God said it, I can stand on it. I can trust His Word. His Word is true. I'm one of those crazy fanatics; I guess you would say, that believes the Word of God. I've tried to think of other people who might have written the Bible; I couldn't think of anyone else. Have you ever thought about that? I don't think there's any human being that could have written a standard this high. You know your wife didn't write it; it says, 'submit to your husbands'. She would've left that out. You know your husband didn't write it; it says, 'love your wife as Christ loved the church'. He would've left that out. That's hard sometimes. You know your kids didn't write it; it says, 'spare the rod, spoil the child'. You know lazy people didn't write it; it says, 'if you don't work, you don't eat'. Every one of us probably would say there are two or three things that, if I'd written the Bible, I'd left those out. If I would've written it, there probably would've have been eight commandments instead of ten. Every one of us has something we would've left out. No human being could've written a standard this high. It's the Word of God.

What I do is find in the Word of God is where it says that I can have the miracle that I'm believing for. A lot of times, I'll take 3 x 5 cards and I'll write those scriptures out and I'll put them up in my office or in my car or on my mirror so when I'm getting ready I'm constantly seeing those scriptures.

A good friend of mine, Pastor Kendall Bridges, made an incredible tape on healing. He is just taking healing scriptures from the Word of God and reading them. You stand on those scriptures, believing God for the healing that you need Him to do in your life. The second thing to do, when you need a miracle, is find the scripture that promises you that you can have the miracle that you are believing for.

MIRACLES

ASK FOR YOUR MIRACLE

CHAPTER THREE

Ask For Your Miracle

The Bible says in Matthew 7, *"...ask and it shall be given unto you"*. You have not because you ask not. It's time that we begin to ask for our miracle. People say, well that's simple, everyone knows you need to ask. Obviously, there are people who didn't because Jesus had to state it in the Word.

It's time that we make a demand on the anointing, on the ability of God. Reach for your miracle. Pursue the miracle that you desire. You'll only pursue what you feel like you qualify for. You remember the story of the woman with the issue of blood. She reached for her miracle. She pressed in and when she touched the hem of His garment He stopped and said, "someone touched me." Someone touched Him for a desired reason. They were asking, they were reaching, pursuing their miracle.

I want you to stop and ask. Sometimes people don't because they don't feel like they qualify for that miracle. You may want a new house, but don't feel like you are worthy of that new house. You will only pursue what you feel like you qualify for. Do not let your poor self-image keep you from what God has for you. You were created in the likeness and image of God.

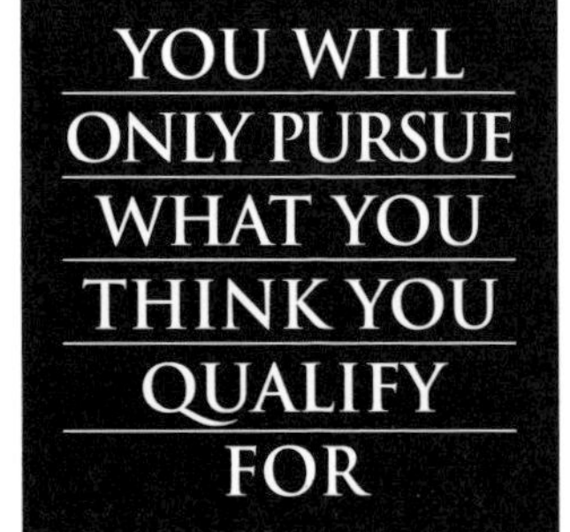

You have got to see yourself worthy of the things God has promised to you. The Israelites didn't leave Egypt until they could see themselves in Cannon. The me I see is the me I will be.

Some people may think to themselves, " I deserve to be this way, I deserve to have this because of what I've done." I know a woman right now in the battle of her life. Her marriage is on the edge of destruction, her children turning to the world, health is in turmoil, and she feels like God will not heal her because of the mistakes in her past. No, that's not what the Bible says. You do not deserve to be sick because you made a mistake in your past. The lie that she is believing is straight from the enemy. He wants you to think you can't have your miracle. If the enemy can convince you of that, you will not ask and if you will not ask, you will not receive.

I want you to stand on Matthew 7 right now and ask for your miracle. The Bible says to ask and you shall receive. You can not receive without *asking*.

You will need to realize that when you ask God for a miracle He will usually give you an instruction. Israel needed a miracle and He told them to walk around Jericho seven days. He gave the blind man *an instruction*. When they needed more wine at the marriage party, Jesus gave *an instruction*.

When you ask God for a miracle, He will give you an instruction. God will never require you to do something impossible. You do the difficult and He will do the impossible. I want you to begin to ask for that miracle and start expecting it to show up.

MIRACLES

GET RID OF DOUBTERS

CHAPTER FOUR

Get Rid Of Doubters

When you're believing God for a miracle, one of the first things you have to do is separate yourself from doubters. Remove yourself from people who don't believe you can have the miracle you are believing for. It's so important that when you're believing God for something that you circle yourself with people that believe the same way you believe.

When I traveled with Pastor Benny Hinn I would see people; some would drive 500 miles to see a miracle and fly 1000 miles to get a miracle. They would get there in an atmosphere of faith. Twenty thousand people, the arena was full; people are believing God and you see people get out of wheel chairs and see growths fall off of people.

With that atmosphere of faith they would reach out and receive their miracle. Then in the next few days as they went back home, some of them went into their homes of doubt and places of unbelief. Some got around people who didn't believe they received what they thought they did..."Maybe you didn't receive that miracle. Maybe you just *think* God did it." As soon as a pain or that first symptom would come on them, they begin to say to themselves, "Well, I *thought* got my healing. Maybe I didn't." By placing yourself around doubters you allow the enemy to put the pain back on you. It's easy to lose your healing once you get it, so it's important that you stay in faith that when the devil does come at you, you can stand strong knowing that you have the miracle that you are believing for.

If I'm trying to start a new business, I don't want to get around people that think I just need to flip hamburgers for the rest of my life. I found out a long time ago that you can't shove a watermelon idea into a pea brain. There are just some people I can not associate with. If I'm ready to go to the next level, there are some people that aren't going to go there with me. So I begin to stretch, to reach up, to grab hold of people that are already at the level that I want to go to. I've got family members; I love them and hug them during Christmas time; don't want to hang out with them. They don't see things like I see things. They don't dream like I dream. They don't believe like I believe and so I don't want to contaminate my thinking and what I'm believing for with negativity and unbelief.

I remember one time when I was pastoring, a gentleman called me on the telephone that attended the church and said, "Pastor, I'm at the hospital, they've given my dad three days to live. I want you to come pray with him and believe with me. I don't believe it's his time to go. I believe God can heal him and I want you to come and pray with me." I said I would be there so I got dressed and went up to the hospital. When I arrived at the hospital his sister walked out the door of the hospital room and said, "Pastor, we're so glad you're here. Mom's just going to be so glad you're here. You know they've just given dad three days to live and any day now he's going to go on and be with the Lord but just the fact of knowing that you're here and knowing that you're with her will mean so much to dad as he goes on to be with the Lord." I thought, that's not what I'm believing for. That's not the reason I got dressed and drove up to the hospital. I came believing for healing. Then the other brother came out of the room and said, "Oh, Pastor, we're so glad you came by. You know they just gave dad a couple of days here and he's going to be going on to be with the Lord and even though he can't talk and communicate with you, just knowing that you were here, I'm sure in his spirit he'll feel better." Again, I thought, that's not the reason I came up here. All of a sudden, Mark, the brother that had called me came out the door and he was ecstatic! He said, "Pastor, I'm so glad you're here! Let's get in there and pray. I believe it's time for dad's healing. Let's get in there and pray right now." I said – that's what I came for! That's the kind of faith I was looking for when I got here. So, he and I walked in the room and as we were walking in I noticed that his brother and sister were following behind us and I said, "Where are you two going." They said, "I thought you were going in to pray" and I said, "I am, but we're going in to pray and believe God for his healing, you believe he's already dead. You think he's already gone. You're just glad I'm here to be with the family. We're believing for healing so you just wait outside in the hallway." Well, they got a little offended. I understand that it upset them a little bit, but I had to remove the doubt and unbelief from my atmosphere of faith. They left the room a little upset, but Mark and I began to pray and we got in agreement and believe God touched heaven for his healing.

You know, three days went by and he wasn't dead yet. A week went by and he was still alive. Two weeks went by and he was sitting up in his bed eating meals, talking to everyone. By the third week, they had discharged him and sent him home. That was over seven years ago and the man is still alive today! Why? Because we *separated ourselves* from those who didn't believe we could have what we were believing for. Sometimes, you're going to have to remove yourself from doubters. Separate yourself from people that can't get in agreement with you for the miracle that you desire.

Doubt is one of the most destructive tools that the enemy can use to keep us from achieving everything that we desire to achieve. I've noticed in church that doubt and negativity keep us so much from achieving what God desires the church to achieve. I used to preach a message on the church's greatest thieves. One thief was Mr. You Can't Make It: "Oh, we shouldn't do that, that's too much for us. We better not try that, that'll be a little more than we can handle. Pastor, you know, we have a small church here. We're only a few years old." I don't like to be around Mr. You Can't Make It. I know you don't either. You want people around you saying, "You can do it! You can make it! You can be it! Whatever you desire." You want people around you, sending you positive messages that you can be a success in life.

I used to think, growing up in church, that if we got all of the sinners out of the church that we'd have a good church. However, I found out it wasn't the sinners that were killing the church, it was church people that were killing the church. Thieves like Mr. Good Enough or Mr. You Can't Make It: "Oh, don't do that, don't try that, you can't make it." No, you want to be around, "you can make it, you can do it, you can accomplish it!"

Don't allow negativity to hold you back from what you desire. You have a choice every morning when you wake up how to start your day, whether to make it positive or make it negative. You decide first thing when you get up.

You wake up and say, "Good Morning Lord!" or you can wake up and say, "Good Lord...Morning." At that point, you decide how you're going to start your day, whether to start it "Good Morning, Lord" and begin to create thoughts of faith. Thoughts that you can make it, you can do it, you can accomplish that, you *will* make that sale that you've been trying to make, the weather *is* beautiful outside. All of those positive, faith-filled, victorious, more-than-a-conqueror thoughts begin to go through your mind.

Or, you wake up in the morning and say, "Good Lord... Morning." and in your mind begins negative thoughts of defeat. Thoughts of discouragement, thoughts of despair, it's a bad day, it's raining outside, your back hurts, your knee hurts, your kids are in a bad mood, you'll never catch up on that work. All of these negative thoughts begin to go through your mind. You choose, each day, whether to bring out the positive or the negative.

This reminds me of these two young boys that decided to play a trick on their grandfather. They snuck into the bedroom where their grandfather was sleeping and they had just come from the kitchen where they got a little bit of Limburger cheese. They cut a piece of Limburger cheese and they put it in the corner of their grandfather's mustache. A few minutes later, he woke up from his nap and sat up in his bed and as he breathed in he said, "My goodness, this room! It stinks in here! I'm going into the living room." He walked down the hall, into the living room and said, "My goodness, it stinks in the living room. I'm going into the kitchen." Finally, he walks in the kitchen and says, "My goodness, the kitchen stinks too. This whole house stinks!" He threw open the front door, walked outside, took a deep breath and said, "My goodness, the whole world stinks!"

Now that's what a lot of people do today. They go around saying the whole world stinks. Why? Because the stink is on them! If the stink is on them, everywhere they go is going to stink. You choose every day whether to bring out the positive or whether to bring out the negative. Make a choice today to surround yourself with positive, uplifting people, thoughts and messages. Remove yourself from doubters!

MIRACLES

DON'T GIVE UP

CHAPTER FIVE

Don't Give Up

I can picture the first day we arrive in Heaven. St. Peter meets us at the gate and says, "Follow me for just a minute." We follow him down a beautiful golden street into this giant warehouse and we walk in the warehouse and he says, "Look around for a minute." We're looking around this warehouse and all of a sudden you say, "Hey, I like that. I wanted one of those one time." Peter says, "Well, that was yours but you gave up!" Could you imagine a warehouse full of all of the things that belonged to us, but we gave up before we received them? We let go and quit believing. We thought we couldn't have it.

A lady came up to me one time and said, "You know, I believed for six months for a new van. I needed a new van and I prayed and prayed, I believed and it never came?" I said, "For six months?" She said, "For six months." I said, "Did you ever think God would give it to you in the seventh month?" She said, "No, I didn't think about that." She may have given up right at the edge of her miracle. I wonder how many times we are at the edge of our miracle, but we give up. We think it's not going to happen, there's no way it's going to happen. We have to hold strong to our faith; not grow weary in well doing for in due season you shall reap if you faint not.

Don't give up! Stand strong. Build yourself up on your most holy faith. Jude verse 20 says to build yourself up on your most holy faith by praying in the Holy Ghost. Sometimes when I don't know what else to do, where else to turn, I just begin to pray and talk to the Holy Spirit and He begins to give me strength and encouragement and the ability to keep standing for the miracle I'm believing for. He gives the ability to not give up, to not turn back, to not begin to speak negatively over the situation. The Holy Spirit is walking beside you every day. He's the best friend you'll ever have and He cares about every decision you make. He's the one that'll help you be at the right place at the right time every day of your life. You might as well get to know Him because you'll never be happy without Him. The Holy Spirit, He left Himself out of everything so that nothing could make you happy without Him. That's why your husband can't make you happy without him; your wife will never make you happy without him. No human being on earth could make you happy without the Holy Spirit. No material thing, no boat, no car, no house will ever make you happy without Him.

I've seen it so many times. In church, I'll see single people sitting, looking across the aisle at a married couple thinking, "Oh, if I was married, I'd be happy, my life would be complete, everything would be wonderful, if I was just married." Then I see married couples looking back across the aisles at single people thinking, "Oh, freedom, freedom, freedom." There's a down side to everything.

You might as well get to know the Holy Spirit because it's through Him you build up your faith by praying and talking to Him, to keep standing until you receive the miracle you're believing for. Don't give up at the edge of your miracle. Oral Roberts said one time, "There are miracles coming to you or going past you every day. All you've got to do is reach out and take hold of the one that belongs to you."

MIRACLES

SEE YOUR MIRACLE

CHAPTER SIX

See Your Miracle

Before you ever see your miracle come to pass in the natural, you're going to have to begin to see it through the eyes of faith. What is it you are believing for in the future? Something has to be see-able before it's believable and believable before it's achievable.

One of the first things I do when I'm believing for a miracle is I begin to see it with my imagination. If I am believing for my brother to get saved, I can close my eyes when I pray and see him sitting next to me in church, see him with his hands lifted, see him worshipping God. If you're believing for your marriage to be restored, see yourself walking into your home and such love, joy and peace in the atmosphere of your home. If you're believing for healing in your body, picture yourself doing what you can't do right now. One of the most powerful keys to receiving your miracle is seeing it through the eyes of faith.

David Yongi Cho pastors the world's largest church in Sole, Korea. For years he preached with his eyes closed. Not because he didn't want to see the people that were there, but because he wanted to picture the thousands that were going to come. At that time, there were only a few people in that auditorium, but when he preached with his eyes closed, he'd picture thousands and thousands that were going to come.

Sometimes, when I wake up in the morning I look at myself in the mirror and say, "Dave, you look better in the future. You look much better than you look right now." Sometimes, I've just got to talk to myself. I can see myself, "Dave you look wealthier in the future. You look much wealthier than you look right now. You look healthier in the future. You look much healthier than you look right now." Sometimes, I turn sideways and say, "Dave, you look skinnier in the future." Begin to talk, begin to see yourself how you want to look in the future.

Many years ago, when I was pastoring a church, sometimes in the middle of the day when no one was in the building, I would go into the sanctuary to the platform and

I would sit and look out across the sanctuary and see empty chairs through my natural eyes, but as I closed my eyes and began to see through the eyes of faith, I could see every chair full. I could see people walking down the aisle to give their heart to God, to make things right in their life. I could see people being restored, healings taking place. I could see that place full of people. That was all through the eyes of faith. As I began to see it through the eyes of faith, it began to come to pass in the natural. Salvations and healings began taking place. Chairs started to fill more and more, until the place was full of people worshipping God, just as I had seen it through the eyes of faith.

Whatever it is you're believing for, I want you just to stop right now. Stop reading and close your eyes. I want you to take a few minutes and picture that miracle happening. Whatever it is you want God to do, I want you to picture it happening right now. That new business, get a picture of the building, get a picture of your business card. If it's your marriage, get a picture of you and your spouse happy and enjoying life. If it's a healing, picture yourself running, leaping, dancing, doing what you can't do right now. If you are suffering from depression, get a picture of yourself full of joy and excitement and happiness.

The me I see is the me I will be. I see myself as a success because that's the way God sees me. It's so important how you see yourself.

There are three ways you can see yourself:

1. The way God sees you
2. The way the Devil sees you
3. The way you see yourself.

When I think of those three ways, I sure don't want to see myself the way the Devil sees me. His photo album is all of my mistakes, all of my failures, all of my bad qualities. Everything I've done wrong. That's how he sees me. I see myself, my own self-portrait, my own self-image is pretty good, but I doubt it's near as good as the image and portrait that God has of me. In God's photo album are all the pictures of my successes, my good qualities, things I've accomplished. His portrait of me is a portrait of perfect success. All of the wrinkles of weakness have been removed; all of the blemishes of failure are gone. The portrait is of perfect success. It's time we begin to see ourselves how God sees us.

MIRACLES

YOUR MIRACLE IS IN YOUR MOUTH

CHAPTER SEVEN

Your Miracle Is In Your Mouth

The Bible says in Proverbs that the tongue has the power of life or death. It's in the power of the tongue. It is so important that we *speak faith*. It is so important that we talk like we've already received our miracle.

When I'm believing for a miracle, my words will describe the miracle I'm believing for. If you need healing in your body, talk like you've already received it. If I'm believing for a family member to get saved, you won't hear me say, "Well, you know I prayed for my dad to get saved for twenty years and he's never gotten saved. You know what, I doubt he's ever going to get saved. If that old man changed, that would be a miracle. I think he's so stuck in his way, I don't think there's much hope for him getting saved." Or you could hear me say, "I can't wait until my dad gets saved. When he gets saved it's going to be awesome to go to church together and talk about the things of God together. That day is coming so soon I can't even wait! I can't wait until that day comes and he gives his heart to God."

Do you see the difference between the things I've said? One was speaking negatively; talking like that miracle was never going to happen. The other was talking about how I couldn't wait. It hadn't happened yet, but any day now, any second now, it was going to take place, that which I was believing for. I'm talking like I've already got the miracle. My words are creating my future, my circumstances.

MIRACLES

PLANTING A SEED

CHAPTER EIGHT

Planting A Seed

What is the biggest need in your life right now?

What miracle is on your mind the most?

What dreams and goals dominate your heart?

Are you facing a situation in your finances?

Do you lay awake at night thinking about unpaid bills?

Do you feel overwhelmed by your present circumstances?

I know how you feel. I have faced many of these same situations and circumstances. That is why I wrote this book. I wanted to share with you the powerful principle that changed my life and produced the answer to many of these questions.

God has already given you enough to create what He has not yet given you.

You always have enough to create more.

What you have in your hand is a Seed. What God has in His hand is a *harvest*. You plant your Seed, in faith, and God will honor it by returning to you the harvest that you desire. I have shown you several examples from God's Word how people sowed Seed for a specific harvest.

One Seed can unleash the miracle you need.

It happened for David. It happened for the Widow at Zarephath, and it can happen for you. Even God understood and used this principle.

God had a desire...a harvest...to have a family. He took His best Seed, which was his only Son, Jesus. He gave His Seed a purpose. The purpose was to seek and save that which was lost. Today, you and I are the harvest. We are the family God desired, a result of His Seed.

The first scripture almost every Christian memorizes is John 3:16:

"For God so loved the world that He gave His one and only Son, that whoever believes in Him shall not perish but have eternal life."

We see in this fundamental scripture the principle of assigning purpose to a Seed. It says that God gave so that we would have eternal life. You too, can create the harvest you desire. You already have in your hand everything it takes to make tomorrow what it should be.

Every seed contains an invisible instruction.

If you were to look deep inside of a tomato seed, you would find an instruction to produce a tomato. Orange seeds contain an instruction to produce oranges. You cannot see it with the natural eye, but it is obviously there.

God decided the harvest when He created the seed.

I can still remember the night I caught this revelation and it sank into my spirit. Dr. Mike Murdock was teaching and he said these words, "When God wanted a family, He sowed His Son. He gave His Son an assignment to seek and save the lost. Jesus was the best Seed God ever planted on earth. He contained an assignment, an instruction, and a purpose. Everything He did was connected to that assignment...everyday of His life."

I saw it! Even God would sow a Seed for a specific harvest. Well, if it worked for God, I thought I should try it. I did. It worked and my life has never been the same again. If in these next few paragraphs you can get a hold of this principle, it will change your life also.

In 2 Samuel 24, we see that David aimed his Seed like an arrow. He gave it an instruction. He focused his faith and expected the desired result. Thousands were dead. Then David brought an offering for a specific thing, and the plague was stopped.

I love the story in 1 Kings 17 about the Widow at Zarephath. The prophet gave her a picture of what God would do for her if she would give him something to eat. She saw the photograph of her harvest before she sowed her Seed. She was sowing for a specific harvest.

"For this is what the Lord, the God of Israel, says:
'The jar of flour will not be used up and the
jug of oil will not run dry until the day
the Lord gives rain on the land.'"
— 1 KINGS 17:14

You always have a Seed that can move you out of your present situation. Your Seed may be your way out of trouble. I have sown Seeds for healing, for favor, for finances, for victory, for marriage, and many more. You know you can't buy a miracle from God. I am not trying to tell you that, but you can sow a Seed with expectation for a desired result.

Your faith must have a specific instruction. Not two. Not three. One. Don't waver. Target your Seed. Sow your Seed consistently, generously, and always in obedience to the voice of God. Then, wrap your faith around your Seed and point it like an arrow.

Enter into a covenant for a specific and desired result in your life. Many fail to do this and never receive the harvest God promised. *"Ye have not, because ye ask not"* (James 4:2, KJV).

Now this is what I want you to do. I am going to give you an opportunity to plant a Seed. I am going to ask you to do three things:

- I want you to listen to the voice of the Holy Spirit and obey what He says.
- I want you to plant a Seed with expectation of a harvest.
- I then want you to give that Seed an assignment.

He may speak to you about $50, $100, $1,000 or even more. Now, I want you to take a step of faith and prove God with an offering. I challenge you right now to plant a Seed.

Ask God what He would have you do. He spoke to a man in Knoxville to sow a $1,000 Seed. A woman in West Virginia He spoke to about $25. He spoke to a woman in Los Angeles to sow $111 and a man in Orlando to sow $10,000. The amount is not as important as the obedience to His voice.

A Seed of nothing will produce a season of nothing.

You are creating your tomorrow today. Your tomorrow is being decided right now. Your Seed may leave your hand, but it will never leave your life. It is on its way to your future where it will multiply and bring forth the harvest you desire.

When God speaks to you about a Seed. He has a harvest on His mind.

Nothing leaves heaven until something leaves earth.

Whatever you put in God's hand will multiply. Do you remember the story of the boy with a few loaves and fishes? All that boy had was a few loaves and fishes until Jesus touched it. When Jesus touched it, there was enough to feed thousands, plus twelve baskets to take home.

If you put nothing in His hand, that will multiply as well. Nothing times nothing equals nothing. I know you can't make it on nothing, and don't want to try to live a day with nothing.

When you give, you are not buying from God. You are worshipping Him through your giving which shows Him that He is your Source. Christine and I want to agree with you for your miracle. Stop right now and plant a Seed for the harvest you need most in your life.

Sow it today—RIGHT NOW! We want to pray the prayer of agreement with you. We are going to come into agreement with you and we are not going to come out of the agreement until we see the answer. I look forward to hearing from you today.

Dave and Christine Martin
Dave Martin International
PO Box 608150
Orlando, Florida 32860
or sow online
www.davemartin.org

MIRACLES

THE MIRACLES OF JESUS

FAITH-BUILDING

BONUS SECTION!

The Miracles of Jesus

TURNING THE WATER TO WINE

The next day Jesus' mother was a guest at a wedding celebration in the village of Cana in Galilee. Jesus and his disciples were also invited to the celebration. The wine supply ran out during the festivities, so Jesus' mother spoke to him about the problem. "They have no more wine," she told him.

"How does that concern you and me?" Jesus asked. "My time has not yet come." But his mother told the servants, "Do whatever he tells you." Six stone waterpots were standing there; they were used for Jewish ceremonial purposes and held twenty to thirty gallons each.

Jesus told the servants, "Fill the jars with water." When the jars had been filled to the brim, he said, "Dip some out and take it to the master of ceremonies." So they followed his instructions.

When the master of ceremonies tasted the water that was now wine, not knowing where it had come from (though, of course, the servants knew), he called the bridegroom over. "Usually a host serves the best wine first," he said. "Then, when everyone is full and doesn't care, he brings out the less expensive wines. But you have kept the best until now!" This miraculous sign at Cana in Galilee was Jesus' first display of his glory. And his disciples believed in him.

— JOHN 2:1-11

THE MIRACULOUS CATCH OF FISH

When he had finished speaking, he said to Simon, "Now go out where it is deeper and let down your nets, and you will catch many fish." "Master," Simon replied, "we worked hard all last night and didn't catch a thing. But if you say so, we'll try again." And this time their nets were so full they began to tear! A shout for help brought their partners in the other boat, and soon both boats were filled with fish and on the verge of sinking. When Simon Peter realized what had happened, he fell to his knees before Jesus and said, "Oh, Lord, please leave me – I'm too much of a sinner to be around you." For he was awestruck by the size of their catch, as were the others with him.

— LUKE 5:4-9

HEALING THE CENTURION'S SERVANT

Now the highly valued slave of a Roman officer was sick and near death. When the officer heard about Jesus, he sent some respected Jewish leaders to ask him to come and heal his slave. So they earnestly begged Jesus to come with them and help the man. "If anyone deserves your help, it is he," they said, "for he loves the Jews and even built a synagogue for us."

So Jesus went with them. But just before they arrived at the house, the officer sent some friends to say, "Lord, don't trouble yourself by coming to my home, for I am not worthy of such an honor. I am not even worthy to come and meet you. Just say the word from where you are, and my servant will be healed. I know because I am under the authority of my superior officers, and I have authority over my soldiers. I only need to say, 'Go,' and they go, or 'Come,' and they come. And if I say to my slaves, 'Do this or that,' they do it."

When Jesus heard this, he was amazed. Turning to the crowd, he said, "I tell you, I haven't seen faith like this in all the land of Israel!" And when the officer's friends returned to his house, they found the slave completely healed.

— LUKE 7:2-10

FEEDING THE FIVE THOUSAND

Jesus soon saw a great crowd of people climbing the hill, looking for him. Turning to Philip, he asked, "Philip, where can we buy bread to feed all these people?" He was testing Philip, for he already knew what he was going to do.

Philip replied, "It would take a small fortune to feed them!"
Then Andrew, Simon Peter's brother, spoke up. "There's a young boy here with five barley loaves and two fish. But what good is that with this huge crowd?" "Tell everyone to sit down," Jesus ordered.

So all of them – the men alone numbered five thousand – sat down on the grassy slopes. Then Jesus took the loaves, gave thanks to God, and passed them out to the people. Afterward he did the same with the fish. And they all ate until they were full.

"Now gather the leftovers," Jesus told his disciples, "so that nothing is wasted." There were only five barley loaves to start with, but twelve baskets were filled with the pieces of bread the people did not eat!

When the people saw this miraculous sign, they exclaimed, "Surely, he is the Prophet we have been expecting!"

— JOHN 6:5-14

WALKING ON THE SEA

Immediately after this, Jesus made his disciples get back into the boat and head out across the lake to Bethsaida, while he sent the people home. Afterward he went up into the hills by himself to pray. During the night, the disciples were in their boat out in the middle of the lake, and Jesus was alone on land.

He saw that they were in serious trouble, rowing hard and struggling against the wind and waves. About three o'clock in the morning he came to them, walking on the water. He started to go past them, but when they saw him walking on the water, they screamed in terror, thinking he was a ghost. They were all terrified when they saw him. But Jesus spoke to them at once. "It's all right," he said. "I am here! Don't be afraid."

Then he climbed into the boat, and the wind stopped. They were astonished at what they saw. They still didn't understand the significance of the miracle of the multiplied loaves, for their hearts were hard and they did not believe.

— MARK 6:45-52

FEEDING THE FOUR THOUSAND

About this time another great crowd had gathered, and the people ran out of food again. Jesus called his disciples and told them, "I feel sorry for these people. They have been here with me for three days, and they have nothing left to eat. And if I send them home without feeding them, they will faint along the road. For some of them have come a long distance."

"How are we supposed to find enough food for them here in the wilderness?" his disciples asked. "How many loaves of bread do you have?" he asked. "Seven," they replied.

So Jesus told all the people to sit down on the ground. Then he took the seven loaves, thanked God for them, broke them into pieces, and gave them to his disciples, who distributed the bread to the crowd.

A few small fish were found, too, so Jesus also blessed these and told the disciples to pass them out. They ate until they were full, and when the scraps were picked up, there were seven large baskets of food left over!

There were about four thousand people in the crowd that day, and he sent them home after they had eaten.

— MARK 8:1-9

HEALING THE BLIND MAN

As Jesus was walking along, he saw a man who had been blind from birth. "Teacher," his disciples asked him, "why was this man born blind? Was it a result of his own sins or those of his parents? "It was not because of his sins or his parents' sins," Jesus answered. "He was born blind so the power of God could be seen in him.

All of us must quickly carry out the tasks assigned us by the one who sent me, because there is little time left before the night falls and all work comes to an end. But while I am still here in the world, I am the light of the world." Then he spit on the ground, made mud with the saliva, and smoothed the mud over the blind man's eyes.

He told him, "Go and wash in the pool of Siloam" (Siloam means Sent). So the man went and washed, and came back seeing! His neighbors and others who knew him as a blind beggar asked each other, "Is this the same man – that beggar?"

Some said he was, and others said, "No, but he surely looks like him!" And the beggar kept saying, "I am the same man!" They asked, "Who healed you? What happened?" He told them, "The man they call Jesus made mud and smoothed it over my eyes and told me, 'Go to the pool of Siloam and wash off the mud.' I went and washed, and now I can see!" "Where is he now?" they asked. "I don't know," he replied.

Then they took the man to the Pharisees. Now as it happened, Jesus had healed the man on a Sabbath. The Pharisees asked the man all about it. So he told them, "He smoothed the mud over my eyes, and when it was washed away, I could see!"

Some of the Pharisees said, "This man Jesus is not from God, for he is working on the Sabbath." Others said, "But how could an ordinary sinner do such miraculous signs?" So there was a deep division of opinion among them. Then the Pharisees once again questioned the man who had been blind and demanded, "This man who opened your eyes – who do you say he is?" The man replied, "I think he must be a prophet."

The Jewish leaders wouldn't believe he had been blind, so they called in his parents. They asked them, "Is this your son? Was he born blind? If so, how can he see?"

His parents replied, "We know this is our son and that he was born blind, but we don't know how he can see or who healed him. He is old enough to speak for himself. Ask him." They said this because they were afraid of the Jewish leaders, who had announced that anyone saying Jesus was the Messiah would be expelled from the synagogue.

That's why they said, "He is old enough to speak for himself. Ask him." So for the second time they called in the man who had been blind and told him, "Give glory to God by telling the truth, because we know Jesus is a sinner." "I don't know whether he is a sinner," the man replied. "But I know this: I was blind, and now I can see!"

"But what did he do?" they asked. "How did he heal you?" "Look!" the man exclaimed. "I told you once. Didn't you listen? Why do you want to hear it again? Do you want to become his disciples, too?" Then they cursed him and said, "You are his disciple, but we are disciples of Moses. We know God spoke to Moses, but as for this man, we don't know anything about him."

"Why, that's very strange!" the man replied. "He healed my eyes, and yet you don't know anything about him! Well, God doesn't listen to sinners, but he is ready to hear those who worship him and do his will. Never since the world began has anyone been able to open the eyes of someone born blind. If this man were not from God, he couldn't do it."

"You were born in sin!" they answered. "Are you trying to teach us?" And they threw him out of the synagogue. When Jesus heard what had happened, he found the man and said, "Do you believe in the Son of Man?" The man answered, "Who is he, sir, because I would like to."

"You have seen him," Jesus said, "and he is speaking to you!" "Yes, Lord," the man said, "I believe!" And he worshiped Jesus. Then Jesus told him, "I have come to judge the world. I have come to give sight to the blind and to show those who think they see that they are blind." The Pharisees who were standing there heard him and asked, "Are you saying we are blind?" "If you were blind, you wouldn't be guilty," Jesus replied. "But you remain guilty because you claim you can see.

— JOHN 9:1-41

RAISING LAZARUS

A man named Lazarus was sick. He lived in Bethany with his sisters, Mary and Martha. This is the Mary who poured the expensive perfume on the Lord's feet and wiped them with her hair. Her brother, Lazarus, was sick. So the two sisters sent a message to Jesus telling him, "Lord, the one you love is very sick."

But when Jesus heard about it he said, "Lazarus's sickness will not end in death. No, it is for the glory of God. I, the Son of God, will receive glory from this." Although Jesus loved Martha, Mary, and Lazarus, he stayed where he was for the next two days and did not go to them.

Finally after two days, he said to his disciples, "Let's go to Judea again." But his disciples objected. "Teacher," they said, "only a few days ago the Jewish leaders in Judea were trying to kill you. Are you going there again?"

Jesus replied, "There are twelve hours of daylight every day. As long as it is light, people can walk safely. They can see because they have the light of this world. Only at night is there danger of stumbling because there is no light." Then he said, "Our friend Lazarus has fallen asleep, but now I will go and wake him up."

The disciples said, "Lord, if he is sleeping, that means he is getting better!" They thought Jesus meant Lazarus was having a good night's rest, but Jesus meant Lazarus had died. Then he told them plainly, "Lazarus is dead. And for your sake, I am glad I wasn't there, because this will give you another opportunity to believe in me. Come, let's go see him."

Thomas, nicknamed the Twin, said to his fellow disciples, "Let's go, too – and die with Jesus." When Jesus arrived at Bethany, he was told that Lazarus had already been in his grave for four days. Bethany was only a few miles down the road from Jerusalem, and many of the people had come to pay their respects and console Martha and Mary on their loss.

When Martha got word that Jesus was coming, she went to meet him. But Mary stayed at home. Martha said to Jesus, "Lord, if you had been here, my brother would not have died. But even now I know that God will give you whatever you ask."

Jesus told her, "Your brother will rise again." "Yes," Martha said, "when everyone else rises, on resurrection day." Jesus told her, "I am the resurrection and the life. Those who believe in me, even though they die like everyone else, will live again. They are given eternal life for believing in me and will never perish. Do you believe this, Martha?"

"Yes, Lord," she told him. "I have always believed you are the Messiah, the Son of God, the one who has come into the world from God." Then she left him and returned to Mary. She called Mary aside from the mourners and told her, "The Teacher is here and wants to see you." So Mary immediately went to him.

Now Jesus had stayed outside the village, at the place where Martha met him. When the people who were at the house trying to console Mary saw her leave so hastily, they assumed she was going to Lazarus's grave to weep. So they followed her there. When Mary arrived and saw Jesus, she fell down at his feet and said, "Lord, if you had been here, my brother would not have died."

When Jesus saw her weeping and saw the other people wailing with her, he was moved with indignation and was deeply troubled. "Where have you put him?" he asked them. They told him, "Lord, come and see."

Then Jesus wept. The people who were standing nearby said, "See how much he loved him." But some said, "This man healed a blind man. Why couldn't he keep Lazarus from dying?" And again Jesus was deeply troubled. Then they came to the grave. It was a cave with a stone rolled across its entrance.

"Roll the stone aside," Jesus told them. But Martha, the dead man's sister, said, "Lord, by now the smell will be terrible because he has been dead for four days." Jesus responded, "Didn't I tell you that you will see God's glory if you believe?"

So they rolled the stone aside. Then Jesus looked up to heaven and said, "Father, thank you for hearing me. You always hear me, but I said it out loud for the sake of all these people standing here, so they will believe you sent me." Then Jesus shouted, "Lazarus, come out!"

And Lazarus came out, bound in graveclothes, his face wrapped in a headcloth. Jesus told them, "Unwrap him and let him go!" Many of the people who were with Mary believed in Jesus when they saw this happen. But some went to the Pharisees and told them what Jesus had done.

— JOHN 11:1-46

CAN I INTRODUCE YOU TO MY BEST FRIEND?

Before you lay this book aside, make sure you put God first so that you can walk in His Favor, Blessings, and Increase and have the desires of your heart.

First, ask Jesus to cleanse you of your sins.You do not have to clean up your life first—God will do that for you. He will also give you a new heart, new desires, and the Spirit of Truth.

If you truly want a change in your life, then pray this prayer out loud and believe:

> *"Father in Heaven, I've heard Your Word, and I want to be born again. Jesus, cleanse me of my sins. I want to be a child of God. I want to give my life to You. Make me a new person. Be my Lord and Savior.*
>
> *I believe I'm now born again, because the Word of God says I am! Jesus is my Lord.Thank you, Jesus, for a new life. Amen!"*

Now do not go by what you feel. Go by what God's Word says.You are saved—you are born again. Believe it!

WE WANT TO HEAR FROM YOU!

If you prayed this prayer sincerely, call us at 407.770.2020 Also, we want to hear your praise reports and testimonies of God's Favor on your life! Write to us at

DAVE AND CHRISTINE MARTIN

P.O. Box 608150 • Orlando, FL 32860

ED YOUNG

"I encourage every pastor to get in touch with Dr. Dave because he will rock your church and take it to a whole *nutha* level in wisdom, success, and finances."

BISHOP HILLIARD

"When Dr. Dave Martin speaks, thousands are affected. He is one of the most prolific and humorous speakers I have ever heard."

JUDAH SMITH

"Dr. Dave will challenge you to look at life different and trust me you will like what you see."

BEN GIBERT

"Dave has an amazing humor that makes learning easy and an ability to motivate those that lack drive, and supercharge the driven to new levels."

BOB HARRISON

"Dave is one of the most powerful and gifted speakers I have ever heard. With skill and humor he drives the points home."

DR. MIKE MURDOCK

"Churches needs his message. Ministers need his wisdom. He will move you to the next level of success."

Keep in touch with live events and ministry in your area!

VIA FACEBOOK
www.facebook.com/drdavemartin

VIA TWITTER
www.twitter.com/drdavemartin

VIA YOUTUBE
www.youtube.com/drfavor